Swiss Family Robinson

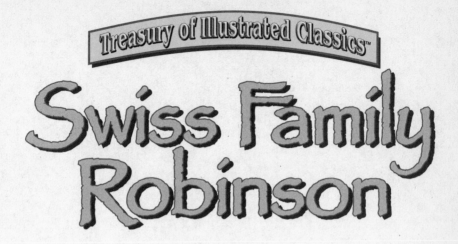

Treasury of Illustrated Classics™

Swiss Family Robinson

by
Johann Wyss

Adapted by
Sara Hoard

Illustrated by
Ned Butterfield

Modern Publishing
A Division of Unisystems, Inc.
New York, New York 10022

Series UPC: 39360

Cover Art by Ned Butterfield

Contents

Chapter 1
A Shipwreck. 9

Chapter 2
Land!. 21

Chapter 3
Exploring. 33

Chapter 4
Return to the Wreck. 47

Chapter 5
Building a Home. 63

Chapter 6
Naming our Lands. 75

Chapter 7
New Discoveries. 93

Chapter 8
    The Anniversary. 111

Chapter 9
    Our Second Winter. 121

Chapter 10
    A Dangerous Visitor. 131

Chapter 11
    A New Land. 139

Chapter 12
    A Great Treasure!. 153

Chapter 13
    A Rescue. 165

Chapter 14
    Conclusion. 175

Chapter 1

A Shipwreck

The storm had been going on for six days. We were so far from the right course that no one on board knew where we were. Our courage was sinking. The masts had been cut down. The boat sprang several leaks and began to fill with water. My four sons, Fritz, Ernest, Jack and young Francis, clung to me in fright. My wife, Elizabeth, wiped the tears from her cheeks. We all fell to our knees and began to pray.

At this moment a cry of, "Land! Land!" was heard through the roaring of the waves. Instantly, the ship struck against a rock. Everyone was thrown down. There was a tremendous cracking as if the ship were going to pieces. The sea rushed in from all sides. The vessel had run aground. It couldn't hold together for long.

The captain called out that all was lost and told the sailors to put out the

lifeboats. The words fell on my heart like a dagger. The children broke out in cries. I tried to calm them, saying that the water had not yet reached us, the ship was near land, and there was still hope.

I went on the deck and a wave threw me down. Another followed, then another. A disaster met my eyes. The

ship was shattered in all directions. The ship's company crowded into the lifeboats, till the boats could not hold one person more. They cut the ropes. I called to them frantically to wait for us, but in vain. The roaring of the sea was too loud and the waves, which rose to the height of mountains, made it impossible for them to return anyway. The boats were driven out of sight.

I took comfort in seeing that the cabin which held my family had been driven upwards between two rocks and was now safe. At the same time, in the distance, I could see through the clouds and the rain several nooks of land.

There was no chance of human help, yet it was my duty to appear calm before my family. "Courage," I cried on entering the cabin. "We will find a way to reach land safely." The children believed me, but Elizabeth saw the anxiety eating away at me.

The storm raged on in full fury.

The planks and beams of the ship separated with horrible crashes. We thought of the life boats and feared they must have sunk under the foaming water.

We prepared a small meal. The boys ate, but Elizabeth and I had little appetite. The children went to bed and, exhausted, soon were snoring soundly. Elizabeth and I sat up, afraid and anxious.

We passed this awful night and welcomed with joy the first gleam of light in the morning. The winds had died down, the sky had become peaceful, and hope throbbed in my chest.

But how would we get to land? Ernest wanted to build a raft.

"That would be a good idea," I answered, "if we had the materials to make one. But come, my boys, look around the ship and see what you can find that might help us."

I checked the supply of food and water. Elizabeth and young Francis visited the animals who had been taken on board at the beginning of the trip. They were sick with hunger and thirst.

My son Jack checked the captain's cabin. Scarcely had he opened the door when two large dogs sprang upon him. They were merely hungry. Jack jumped on the larger dog's back. I laughed and praised his courage, but told him to be gentle with the animals. He called the dogs Turk and Flora.

By and by, my little company assembled around me, and each boasted of what he had to contribute. Fritz had

two guns, some gun powder, and some
shot and bullets. Ernest produced
nails, a hatchet, a hammer, and other
tools. Even Francis had a large box
filled with what he called "some little
sharp-pointed hooks."

"Good!" I said. "Francis has
brought the most valuable item—a box
of fishhooks!"

Elizabeth said, "On board are a cow,
a donkey, two goats, six sheep, lambs,
and a pregnant pig. I've fed them all."

"Excellent," I said, "except for Jack, who has brought two dogs, which will no doubt want to eat more than we have to give them."

"Ah," replied Jack, "but if we can get to land, you will see that they will help us in hunting."

"True," I said. "But tell me. How are we to get to land?"

"It can't be difficult," said Jack. "Look at these large tubs. Why can't each of us get into one and float there?"

"It is worth a try. Quick, then, boy! Give me the saw."

I remembered seeing some empty casks in the ship's hold. We hoisted them onto the lower deck, which was by now scarcely above water. I instantly began sawing them in two. In a short time I had produced eight tubs. I viewed them with delight, but my wife sighed deeply as she looked at them. "Never, never," cried she, "can I venture into one of these."

"Not so fast," I said. "My plan is not yet complete."

I then found a long plank and placed my eight tubs on it. We nailed the tubs to the plank and added more planks. When we finished, we'd made a narrow boat, divided into eight compartments.

But now we discovered that the boat was so heavy, we couldn't lift it. I told Fritz to find a crowbar. In the meantime, I sawed a thick round pole into several pieces to make some rollers. I then easily raised the front of the boat,

while Fritz placed the rollers under it. To our great joy, we succeeded in rolling the boat into the water.

We had spent the day hard at work and it was already late. We couldn't have reached land that evening, so we had to spend a second night in the wrecked vessel, which at every instant threatened to fall to pieces.

I tied the life jackets made of casks around my three youngest sons and my wife in case the storm should return. One and all crept into our separate hammocks. Now more calm and hopeful than the day before, a sound sleep prepared us for the next day's labors.

Chapter 2

Land!

By daybreak we were all awake, for we were too hopeful to remain asleep. I said, "The first thing to do is to give each animal on board a hearty meal. We will put out enough food for a few days. We can't take them with us now, but we'll try to return and fetch them later. Are you all ready?"

We loaded our little boat with guns and gun powder, shot and bullets, a chest containing dried soup, another full of hard biscuit, an iron pot, a fishing rod, a chest of nails, another filled with tools, and lastly, some sailcloth to make a tent. We put ten hens and two roosters into one of the tubs. We set the geese, ducks, and pigeons free, hoping they'd fly or swim towards the land. Lastly, my wife loaded a large bag into one of the tubs. We had so many things that we had to leave some behind.

In the first tub sat my wife. In the second, our youngest son Francis, a lovely boy of six, sweet and happy. In the third, Fritz, almost fifteen years of age, a handsome, curly-haired boy full of intelligence and activity. Next came

Jack, a light-hearted, daring lad ten years old. Then came our son Ernest, twelve years old, thoughtful and smart but somewhat lazy. Lastly, I, who would steer the boat with a makeshift rudder. Each one of us held an oar and near each was a life jacket made of casks. We felt prepared for anything, and we set sail.

The boys devoured with their eyes the land they saw at a distance. We rowed with all our strength. The two dogs, seeing that we had abandoned them, plunged into the sea and swam to

our boat. They were too large for us to let them get in, and I feared they might jump in and upset the boat. What was more, I thought they wouldn't be able to swim so far. The dogs, however, managed quite well. When tired, they rested their forepaws on one of the paddles, then swam on.

We proceeded safely, though slowly. The nearer we got to the land, the more gloomy it looked. It seemed barren and rocky. But as we got closer, the shore's rough outline softened. Fritz, with his hawk eyes, saw some palm trees. Ernest said happily that we'd get much larger and better coconuts than we'd ever seen before.

By and by, we came upon a little opening in the rocky shore, toward the mouth of a creek. Our geese and ducks had already taken this route, so I followed in their course. This opening formed a little bay. The water was calm, and neither too deep nor too shallow for our boat. We rowed into the nook until the boat gently glided up onto the shore.

We all jumped eagerly on land. The dogs, who had already gone ashore, leaped around us in joy. The geese, ducks, roosters and hens kept up a loud cackling. The boys chattered all at once. To this was added the screams of flamingos, which sat on the rocks at the entrance of the bay.

We quickly unloaded the boat and found a place to set up a tent under the shade of the rocks. I sent my sons to look for grass and moss to make beds. I built a little kitchen near the tent. A few flat stones served as a hearth. I collected some dry branches and made a brisk, cheering fire. We put some of the dried soup with water into our iron pot and made dinner.

Suddenly, I heard loud cries. It was Jack, in trouble. I grabbed my hatchet and ran to help him. He was on his knees in shallow water and a large lobster had

fastened its claws to his leg. The poor boy screamed and tried to shake the lobster free, but couldn't. I jumped into the water. As I jumped in, the lobster let go and would have scampered out to sea. But I grabbed it and carried it off, followed by Jack, who shouted in triumph all the way.

Ernest, always thinking of a good meal, said to put the lobster in the soup, which would give it an excellent flavor. But his mother said no, that we had little food and that the lobster could make a whole dinner for the entire family. I complimented Jack on being the first to find something good to eat.

"Ah, but *I* found something too," said Ernest, "oysters! And I would have gotten them, too, if they hadn't been in the water so I'd have to get wet to catch them."

"Well, go and get them," I said. "In a situation like ours, every member of the family must help out. No one can be afraid of something as small as wet feet."

"I'll do my best," said Ernest, setting off.

But our problems soon increased. "Look," said Elizabeth. "I have made the soup, but how will we eat it without spoons or dishes? We can't each raise this boiling pot to our lips."

We all looked at the pot in confusion. Then, we burst into a hearty laugh at the thought of our problem. Ernest said, "We can use oyster shells for spoons."

"Why, this is a useful idea, Ernest. Run and get some," I said.

As Ernest and Jack did just that, we heard Fritz returning from his own exploring. He held his two hands behind him.

"What have you brought?" asked his brothers.

But Jack didn't wait for an answer and stole behind him. "A suckling pig! A suckling pig!" he cried. Fritz held it up for everyone to see. In fact, it was an agouti and not a pig at all.

Fritz told us that he had passed over to the other side of a river. "Ah," he said. "The shore is low, and many casks and chests and planks have been washed ashore by the sea. Shouldn't we try to collect some of them?"

"Patience," I said. "There's a time for everything. But above all, did you see any trace of our ship's companions?"

"Not the smallest sign," replied Fritz.

We took our meal as the sun began to sink. Our flock of hens gathered around us, pecking morsels of biscuits that had fallen. Elizabeth produced the bag she had mysteriously put into the boat. She opened it and pulled out various grains. She scattered some for the hens and they eagerly began to eat. Our pigeon roosted among the rocks. The geese and ducks took to a marshy bit of ground near some sheltering bushes by the sea.

We too began our preparations to sleep. With the last rays of the sun, we entered our tent and laid ourselves down on the moss and grass. Each of us slept soundly, happy to be together and safe on land at last.

Chapter 3

Exploring

Elizabeth and I were roused at the dawn of day by the crowing of the roosters. The children soon woke, too. Even our lazy Ernest submitted to the hard fate of rising so early in the morning. For breakfast we had lobster from the night before. Fritz and I prepared to explore the area and to look for any traces of our lost shipmates. We took hunting sacks, hatchets, guns, biscuits and fresh river water. The others would remain near the boats, which would offer a speedy escape in case of danger.

We all worried about what new trouble

might occur on either side during our separation. We all melted into tears. As we left, our family's sobs and goodbyes died away in the noise of the waves. Our faithful dog Turk followed after us.

The banks of the river were steep and difficult to cross, except at one narrow pass. On the other side was an unbroken

line of sharp, high rocks. We found some
stones which had fallen into the riverbed.
By stepping upon these and making some
hazardous leaps, we reached the other
side. We climbed the rocks and passed
through some tall, tough, half-dried grass.
There were a great many kinds of trees
everywhere. We kept our eyes cast toward

the smooth sea, looking for our ship-mates, but we saw nothing of them.

We rested under a tree by a stream, listening to birds singing in the trees. Fritz found a coconut on the ground and we ate it, which meant we could save the food we'd brought along. It was a very old coconut, but this was no time to be choosy. We made a hearty meal of it and continued on.

In the forest we came upon some strange trees. Bottle gourds grew from their trunks. I knew that the thick rind of the fruit could be used to make plates, dishes, and flasks. Fritz jumped for joy. "How happy Mother will be!" he said.

I taught my son how to split the gourds and shape them. We soon completed two large plates and a few more small ones. I explained that we must leave the plates to dry in the sun. We'd pick them up on our return trip home. We filled them with sand to keep them from shrinking or warping. Then we went on.

After a walk of about four leagues, we arrived at a spit of land that reached far out into the sea. On it was a tall hill. We climbed it with much effort and sweat. At the top, we could see in all directions. It was a scene of wild, lonely beauty. There was no trace of any human being. Filled with sadness, we lost hope for the other sailors.

We descended the hill and made our way through a wood of palms. We went slowly, fearing at every step that a snake might bite us. I cut a reed-stalk to serve as a club. As I did, a thick sap poured from its end. I tasted it and found it sweet and pleasant. These were sugarcanes! I ate the sap and felt refreshed and strengthened. Fritz tasted it joyfully. What a pleasure it would be to bring some back for the others! Fritz cut at least a dozen of the largest canes and dragged them along.

We returned to the palm wood safely. Here we stretched our legs in the shade and finished our meal. We were scarcely settled when we spied large monkeys in the topmost branches of the coconut trees. They were terrified of the sight of us and the barking of Turk. From the heights, they fixed their eyes on us, grinding their teeth, making horrible grimaces and screaming.

I thought we might get some of the fresh coconuts from the monkeys. I threw some stones though I couldn't make them reach half the height of the monkeys. It didn't matter. The monkeys imitated me. They tore off the coconuts and hurled them down on us.

With difficulty, we avoided the blows. But in a short time, many coconuts lay on the ground around us. Fritz laughed at our success. When there were no more coconuts left to throw, we set about collecting them. We split them between us and continued on our way home.

Poor Fritz complained of being tired. "I never would have thought a few

sugarcanes and coconuts could be so heavy. Yet how glad I'll be when my mother and brothers are tasting them!"

When we reached the place where we had left our gourd plates, we found them perfectly dry. We put them in our hunting bags and went on. As we passed through the wood, Turk sprang upon a troop of monkeys who were skipping about and amusing themselves. They fled, but a young one hid himself in the grass and the dog seized it.

Fritz flew like lightning to the rescue. The monkey sprang nimbly on Fritz's shoulders, and fastened his feet in Fritz's hair. Fritz squawked and shook the monkey, but could do nothing to make him let go. I ran to them, laughing, because the animal was too young to do any harm. With a little gentleness, I succeeded in making him release my son. I took the creature in my arms as one would an infant. He was no larger than a kitten.

"What shall I do with you, poor orphan?" I cried. "If I take you with me, how will I feed you? We already have more mouths to fill than food to put into them."

"Father," cried Fritz. "Do let me have this little monkey. Who knows—his instincts may one day help us to discover some good fruits." I agreed and we resumed our journey. The monkey jumped on Fritz's shoulders. I carried the sugarcanes and coconuts.

We soon found ourselves on the riverbank across from our family. Flora announced our approach by barking and Turk replied heartily. Our much-loved family appeared, with demonstrations of joy at our safe return.

Elizabeth was pleased with everything we'd brought. We, too, were pleased when we saw the excellent meal she had cooked. She had created a turn-spit from some wood she'd found and used it to roast a goose. Its fat ran into some oyster shells which served as a

dripping pan. Little Francis helped out by turning the spit. There was also a dish of fish, which the little ones had caught. The iron pot was bubbling with good-smelling soup. By the side of these stood one of the casks we had recovered from the sea. My wife had knocked the head out to find a cargo of fine Dutch cheeses.

We sat on the ground as Elizabeth put everything on our new dishes. My sons opened the coconuts, ate them, and then made some spoons with the fragments of the shells.

By the time we had finished our meal, the sun was setting. We returned to the grassy mattresses in our tent, shaping some of the moss into a bed for the monkey. Feeling peaceful, we retired and soon fell into a deep and refreshing sleep.

Chapter 4

Return to the Wreck

The next morning I told Elizabeth, "We must make a journey to the wrecked ship. We can bring back the cow and other important things. From moment to moment we risk losing these because of a few big waves. On the other hand, we must also build a better home, secure from wild beasts. I don't know what to do first."

Elizabeth replied, "I shudder at the thought of this voyage to the vessel because it's dangerous. But if it's necessary, it must be done quickly."

"I will follow your advice," I said.

Fritz and I would go. There was much to do so we would spend the night on board. We readied our makeshift boat and set off in silence, both of us rowing. After great effort, we found ourselves at the vessel, fastened our boat securely to one of its timbers, and got out.

First, Fritz went on the main deck to feed the animals. Then we talked about what to do next. To my surprise, Fritz suggested making a sail for our boat.

"But we have so many other important things to do," I said.

"I found it very difficult to row for so long, Father," Fritz explained. "On our way back, the current will be against us and our boat will be very heavy when it's fully loaded. I'm afraid I won't be strong enough to row back to land."

"Ah, ha!" I said. "There is good sense in what you say. We'll make your sail."

I helped Fritz carry poles for a mast and sailyard. Then I went to the sail room on the damaged ship and cut a

large sail down to size. We also made a rudder and some oars.

We spent the rest of the day loading our little boat with useful objects. The ship had many of the things we needed most. We took nails, cloth, tools, knives, forks and spoons, and a complete assortment of kitchen utensils and pots. We found a strong telescope in the captain's cabin. We secured as much gun powder and shot as we could for catching animals and defending ourselves against wild beasts. I took sacks of corn, wheat, other grain, and some potatoes. Another prize was a chest of choice eatables, including ham and sausage. Fritz reminded me that sleeping on the ground had been both cold and uncomfortable and suggested some hammocks and blankets. We also took ropes, string, and a large roll of sailcloth.

There was a chest containing dozens of young plants of every species of European fruits, which had been carefully packed in moss for the ship's voyage. I saw pear, plum, almond, peach, apple, apricot, chestnut trees and vine shoots. There were sacks full of maize and oats and a handmill for grinding grains. I took a saw mill, two harpoons, and two cannons which had been mounted on the side of the ship. There was even a box of European books, which I held dear. In short, we'd have everything we needed to start a small colony.

But by far, our greatest prize was a beautiful little sailboat, called a pinnace, which had been taken apart and stored in the hull of the ship. It took us the better part of a day to put it together and then to launch it into the water. But when we were done, we had a wonderful vehicle for sailing.

There were so many valuable things, but we couldn't take all of them. We'd have to leave much behind. But Fritz was already thinking about a second trip to

the vessel. However, it was in such terrible condition that the smallest storm would make it go to pieces, and we weren't sure we could ever go near it again.

The day had been filled with hard work, and night soon surprised us. A large blazing fire on the land greeted our sight. It was the signal from our family to assure us all was well. We tied four lanterns to our masthead as an answer: All was well with us, too. Then we slept.

Early the next morning, though it was scarcely light, I looked through the telescope, hoping to see our beloved family on shore. Elizabeth was coming from the tent, looking toward the vessel. The flag on shore told me that all were in good health and had remained safe through the night.

"Now that I have had a sight of your mother," I said to Fritz, "my next concern is for the animals. Let's take some with us."

We knew it would be too difficult to make a raft which would sail them to shore. We solved our problem by tying swimming jackets made of cork around each animal.

The animal that we lowered into the water was a little lamb. As we watched it sink, I began to fear that it would drown, but then it reappeared, shaking the water from its head. In a few seconds it had learned completely the art of swimming.

"Victory!" I exclaimed, hugging my boy with delight.

We lost not a moment in making more cork jackets, which we tied onto each animal—cow, donkey, goats, lamb, and pig. Then we tied a length of cord around each animal so we'd be able to draw them along behind our boat. Then we brought them near the edge of the vessel and shoved them off. They swam with grace.

We had to work quickly now. We put on our cork jackets and got into our boat. Once we fastened the cords securely to the boat, we drew the animals after us. Finally, we hoisted our sail which, filling with a favorable wind, bore us toward the land. We were proud of our success at so incredible a feat!

But my thoughts were interrupted when Fritz exclaimed, "Help! Now we're lost! A huge shark!"

"Why lost?" said I, half angry and yet half as frightened as he. "Be ready with your gun."

The shark had nearly reached the boat, and with the speed of lightning had seized one of the goats. Fritz aimed and fired skillfully. The shark swam away, staining the water red with its blood.

With the shark went our fears, and the wind drove us straight toward the bay. We found a convenient spot for the animals to land and they stepped happily on shore. Our trip thus ended, we followed their example.

Ernest and Jack ran to the boat and began to shout how much they admired the mast and sail. In the meantime, we began to unpack our cargo. Jack took off the swimming jackets from the sheep and goats, bursting from time to time into shouts of laughter at how ridiculous they looked.

Seeing that there was no dinner cooking, I told Fritz to bring the ham

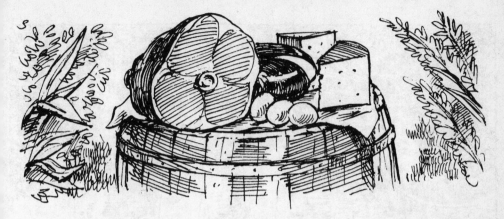

we'd gotten from the ship. "A ham!" cried one and all. "What a great supper we'll have!" And they clapped their hands.

Elizabeth insisted that she hadn't forgotten dinner at all. She showed us about a dozen turtle eggs and then hurried off to make them as a side dish for our ham.

"We found them on the sands along the shore," said Ernest.

"But that is all part of our story," Elizabeth interrupted. She spread a tablecloth on the end of a cask and laid out the ham, eggs, and some cheese. It was a lovely sight. As we ate, Elizabeth told her story.

"This morning, I looked about in hopes of finding a shady place where we might get out of the heat of the sun. But I found not a single tree. This made me think hard. It would be impossible, I said to myself, to remain in this place with no shelter but a miserable tent—the heat was even worse inside it than out in the open.

"Courage, then, I thought. I must explore and find something better. Why not do just that with my younger sons? I will pass over with them to the other side of the river and find some well-shaded spot in which to settle.

"The boys agreed excitedly. We equipped ourselves and started off. We went on until we reached a little wood. Birds were skipping and warbling on the branches of the trees, without being alarmed by us in the least. The trees were enormous, dear husband! Their roots formed great, shaded arches on the ground. A charming, cool stream flowed at our feet and we drank from it.

It occurred to me that if we could create a kind of tent in one of the trees, we might live there safely.

"On our return trip home, we found pieces of timber and chests from the wreck. We weren't strong enough to bring them back, but we dragged them onto the sand, beyond the reach of the waves.

"Meanwhile, our dog Flora was turning over something she had found in the sand. They were the turtle's eggs. We collected nearly two dozen of them. That was when you returned. We ran eagerly toward the river and soon arrived at the shore, where we had nothing further to do but throw ourselves into your arms!"

Chapter 5

Building a Home

The next morning brought new challenges. Elizabeth wanted to move to the tall trees of the forest immediately, while I felt we should first build a bridge over the river. This way, we could cross over easily with all our animals and belongings.

"A bridge!" exclaimed my wife. "But the donkey and cow will carry everything we own on their backs."

"Yes, but they'll have to swim across the river and everything will get wet. We must build the bridge."

The new project would require

planks and timber, which I could only get from the wrecked vessel. I prepared the boat for another journey. This time, I took with me Ernest as well as Fritz so we could finish our work in a shorter time.

We rowed stoutly until we were beyond the bay, but scarcely had we passed a little islet when we saw a great number of seagulls and other birds. I wondered what could have attracted them and steered for the spot.

I brought the boat to anchor with a heavy stone and we stole softly up to the birds. They surrounded an enormous fish, which had been thrown there by the sea. "I believe," said I, "that this is the very shark Fritz wounded yesterday."

"Yes, yes, it's the same one," said my young hero, skipping about for joy.

I saw lying on the ground some planks and timbers. They had been ripped from the ship and driven here by the current. These would do well for our bridge. We bound the planks together

like a raft and tied them to the end of the boat. In four hours, we were ready to return home, without having to risk boarding the wrecked ship.

We once more landed safely on our shore, and unloaded all we had brought from the islet. But how would we get one end of the timber across the stream so that it would lay over the water?

First, I attached a cord to one end of a long plank. I then tied this cord around the trunk of a tree on our own side of the bank. I then fastened a second cord to the other end of the plank and harnessed the donkey and cow to it. Finally, I sent the animals running. As they moved across the stream, they drew one end of the timber to the opposite bank. When the plank lay across the water, Fritz and Jack leaped on it and, in spite of my fatherly fears, crossed the stream joyfully. It was a narrow but effective bridge.

The first timber being thus laid, the rest was much easier. A second and

third were fixed. We laid some short planks across them, and our bridge was completed. By now, we were too tired to do anything more that day. The evening was beginning to set in and we returned to our home, where we ate an excellent lobster dinner and went to bed.

As soon as we were up and had breakfasted the next morning, I directed my family to load the animals with sacks, including tools, kitchen utensils, plates,

and hammocks. We packed and placed in the tent for safekeeping everything we were to leave behind.

Elizabeth said, "We must not leave my enchanted bag," she said smiling, "for who can tell what may yet pop out of it?"

I placed our little Francis on the donkey's back, for he was too small to walk so far, fixing the enchanted bag behind him. Elizabeth led the way with Fritz, then came the cow and donkey, next the goats conducted by Jack. The little monkey, which Jack had named Master Knips, was seated on his back. After Jack came Ernest, conducting the sheep. I brought up the rear. The dogs pranced back and forth as if accompanying a troop of soldiers.

At last, we arrived at the place of the giant trees. The lowest branches were some forty feet in the air! "Good heavens! What trees! What heights! What trunks!" exclaimed one and all.

They were tall fig trees with sweet,

good fruit. As the fruit ripened, they would attract birds. We could hunt these and furnish our table with dishes fit for a nobleman. I gave the boys permission to hunt to their hearts' delight.

"My dear wife, it was you who discovered this beautiful place," I said. "We will fix a tent large enough for all of us in one of these trees, which will keep us safe from wild beasts and provide us with many comforts." I singled out the highest fig tree for our home.

While our dinner was cooking, I made some arrows. I found some stalks of bamboo and used their hard, pointed ends to serve for the tips. Then I attached some bird feathers to the end to make them fly straight.

I now set Fritz and Ernest to work measuring our stock of thick ropes. These would help us to build a ladder so we could climb high into the trees. I tied a strong cord to the end of one of my arrows and shot it so that it would hang over one of the largest branches of our tree. We would then be able to raise our ladder by attaching it to the cord and drawing it up once it was completed.

We all set to work eagerly. Ropes would serve as sides of the ladder, and pieces of sugarcane would be nailed in as rungs. It didn't take long to complete it, and we looked on it with joy and astonishment. I then tied it to the cord which hung from the tree and pulled the far end until our ladder had reached the branch. Everyone shouted joyously.

All the boys wished to be the first to climb it, but I decided it should be Jack, since he was the nimblest. His brothers and I held the ends of the cord with all our strength so the ladder would not fall down (we had yet to tie it to the topmost branch). Our young adventurer tripped up the sugarcane steps with perfect ease. Soon, he took his post on the branch and tied the rope firmly to the tree. It was now

night, and we gathered together for dinner, spread our hammocks in the tall roots of the tree, and fell asleep.

The next morning, we had breakfast and fell to work building a treehouse. We drew the necessary wood up to the heights of the branches by means of a pulley. We used these planks to form walls and a floor. I then made a sailcloth roof, which I spread on the thick branches above. It hung down on the sides and I nailed it to the walls.

At last, we were finished. We unhooked our hammocks from the roots and, using the pulley, hoisted them up the tree. They were soon hung on the branches and everything was ready for the evening. We still had some planks remaining, so we set to building a large table and benches in the large spaces between the roots of the tree. This would be our dining parlor.

In our new home I felt as though we were in one of the strong castles of the ancient cavaliers, with a drawbridge for safety. We ate and then slept, our hearts peaceful and our bodies tired.

Chapter 6

Naming our Lands

"**W**hat do you think, my good family" I said, "of giving names to our home and to the different parts of this country?" They all exclaimed joyfully that the idea was excellent.

Fritz: "Let us call the bay *Oyster Bay*. You remember the oysters we found in it."

Jack: "Oh, no. Let it be called *Lobster Bay* because a large one caught hold of my leg."

Elizabeth: "Out of gratitude, we ought to call it *Bay of Safety*."

Father: "Very good! It shall be *Bay of Safety*. What name shall we give to the spot where we first set up our tent?"

Fritz: "*Tent House*."

Ernest: "And the islet at the entrance of the bay should be called *Shark Island*, for we found that animal there. And this place we have built in the trees should be *Tree Castle*."

Father: "Rather let us call it *The Falcon's Nest*, because falcons make their nests in large trees. The spit of land where Fritz and I looked for sign of

our ship's companions should be called *Cape Disappointment*. The bridge I would name *Family Bridge*."

All agreed, clapping their hands. "Yes, yes!" they cried.

As the day advanced and the intense heat cooled, I invited my family to take a walk. We decided to go across the river to Tent House, then return with new provisions by way of Family Bridge.

On our return trip we were tired, but the scenery was beautiful. We found prickly pears (good for eating), aloe plants (a strong medicine), cactus plants, and the king of fruits—the pineapple, which we all ate with pleasure. I was also fortunate to discover growing in the clefts and at the foot of rocks the karata plant, which can be used for tinder or to make a strong kind of thread.

I demonstrated the plant's usefulness to my sons. I took out my flint and, striking it against the karata, instantly created a fire. The boys looked

on with astonishment, and soon began to caper about exclaiming, "Long live the tinder tree!"

Next, I showed Elizabeth the excellent red "thread" which grew on the underside of the leaves. "How fortunate it is for us," she said, "that you have read and studied so much!"

We continued on our way to Tent
House. Upon arriving, we immediately
loaded up many of the things we had left
behind to return with them to The
Falcon's Nest. However, there were
things which were too heavy to carry,
and I thought I should make a vehicle
for their transportation. I had decided

on Ernest for my assistant, thinking that his lazy temper needed hard work as a cure. We fashioned a sled out of planks of wood and branches.

We harnessed the donkey and the cow to our sled and returned to Tent House to bring back more provisions. The labors of the day had tired us more than usual. We mounted our ladder at an early hour and were soon asleep.

I encouraged my sons to exercise regularly and practice the shooting of arrows, for it was important to increase their strength and agility. They practiced running, jumping, and getting up trees both by climbing the trunks and shinnying up a rope as sailors do to get to the masthead.

I also devised a new weapon in which two heavy stones are tied, one on each end of a cord. These my sons could use to wound an enemy or an animal by flinging one of the ends of the cord at it and instantly drawing back the other.

But if they wished to take the animal alive, and without hurting it, they could throw it in such a way as to make one end run several times round the neck and the other end tangle the animal's legs so that it couldn't run. Fritz soon became quite an expert.

We put many things in order at Falcon's Nest. A pair of young pigeons had recently hatched and were beginning to try their wings. Their mother was already sitting on new eggs. We planted the seedlings of the fruit trees which we had rescued from the ship. We captured a huge female bird called a bustard, though only after a great struggle, and only once had I thought to throw my pocket handkerchief over her eyes so that she could not see to fight. We made additional gourd vessels, for we needed dishes to hold water, collect milk, carry eggs and the like. Fritz and Jack also used the gourds to make nests for the pigeons and hens.

One day, Fritz and I took Turk to do some exploring. As we walked, we picked up some acorns. Different birds of exquisite plumage flitted about us. One was a blue jay, and the others were parrots—red or green and yellow.

We next entered a pretty little grove. I recognized American candleberry trees, which were loaded with large quantities of berries. These, when boiled, would yield a waxlike substance which, happily, we could use to make candles.

Nearby were some unusual trees which resembled the wild fig tree. A kind of gum issued from the trunk and became immediately hardened by the air. Fritz took some, thinking it might work well as a cement or varnish.

As he walked, he frequently looked at his gum, which he tried to soften with his breath, but without success. However, he discovered that the substance stretched. It was rubber! This was indeed a valuable discovery. It could be used to make shoes and boots. Having made many exciting additions to our stores, we turned around and began traveling toward home.

On the following day, Elizabeth and the boys begged me to begin making candles with the candleberry wax. I worked hard to remember all I had read on the subject. I put as many

berries as possible into a vessel and set it on a moderate fire. Elizabeth in the meantime made some wicks with the threads of sailcloth.

When we saw an oily wax of a pleasing smell and light green color rise to the top, we carefully skimmed it off and put it into a separate vessel, taking care to keep it warm. We next dipped the wicks one by one into it and then hung them on the bushes to harden. We repeated the operation until the candles had become big all around.

But there was far more to do that day. I had a great desire to explore the part of the island around Cape Disappointment. The entire family set out with me in full procession. We brought with us tools, food, and water in a gourd-flask.

It was not long before we reached the magnificent bay formed by the cape, which stretched far out into the sea. It was now evening, and we decided to spend the night in this enchanting spot. We built a little hut out of some large tree branches.

But we were suddenly roused by the loud braying of the donkey. It was throwing its head in the air and kicking and prancing about. Then it set off at a full gallop. We sent the dogs after it, but they couldn't catch it. It was too dark to follow it. We decided to chase it in the morning, hoping it would not go too far.

The following morning, we break-fasted on some milk from the cow, some

boiled roots, and some Dutch cheese from the ship. Then Jack and I went after the donkey. We spent an hour following its tracks, until we came to a tall ridge of rocks. We could find no way around it or over it. It separated our part of the island from we knew not what. There was only a narrow passage between the rocks and the river, and we decided the donkey had probably gone this way.

We were curious as to what lay beyond the rocks—land or water. We passed through, then leaped on rocks across a deep, rapidly flowing stream. On the other side we found land—and the donkey's footprints in the earth. They soon petered out and we were sure we would never find the animal again. It was a great loss.

But we also saw with astonishment the prints of other animals, much larger than the donkey. We were so curious that we decided to follow the traces. They brought us to a distant, peaceful and beautiful plain.

By straining our eyes as far as we could see, we noticed some moving specks. We hurried toward them to find a herd of wild buffaloes! I was frightened. But the buffaloes stood perfectly still with their large round eyes fixed on us in vacant surprise. None of them seemed hostile.

All was well, until Turk and Flora caught up with us. The buffaloes became terrified of the dogs and instantly set up such a roar as to make our nerves tremble. They struck their horns and their hoofs upon the ground. Our brave Turk and Flora, fearless of danger, ran into the middle of the buffalo pack and grabbed onto the ears of a young buffalo. And though the animal roared tremendously and kicked with its hoofs, the dogs held fast.

Our only hope of safety was to frighten the buffaloes with our firearms. We fired. The buffaloes, terrified by the sound and the smoke, remained for an

instant motionless, as if struck by a thunderbolt. Then one and all took flight until they were gone. The young buffalo still remained a prisoner of the dogs. I hoped to tame this captive and make it a substitute for the lost donkey. I attached a ring to its nose so I could lead it, and we turned around to rejoin our family. We repassed the river and went through the narrow rock passage. Soon, we were back at the hut.

The next day we began our homeward trip. On our way, we loaded up our cart and the buffalo with more berries, wax, and rubber. When, after so many adventures, we arrived at Falcon's Nest, we experienced what is so often true—that home is dear and sacred to the heart. Our animals welcomed our return in their own noisy, happy manner.

Chapter 7

New Discoveries

The next day, we began some business which Elizabeth and I had been thinking of for some time. She found it difficult and even dangerous to climb up and down the Falcon's Nest tree with a rope ladder. A staircase on the outside, however, was unthinkable as the tree was too high and I didn't have long enough beams. But I had for some time thought of building a winding staircase within the huge trunk of the tree. I had heard the boys talking of a hollow in our tree, so I thought it might be completely hollow.

The boys helped me examine it. They climbed to the top of the tree's gigantic roots like squirrels and struck at the trunk with axes. From the sounds, it seemed thoroughly hollow. But they soon paid dearly for their attempt. A whole swarm of bees, alarmed at the noise, buzzed forth with fury. The boys were stung and soon ran off, crying terribly.

Elizabeth and I covered their wounds with earth to take away the smart. The bees, in the meantime, were still buzzing angrily around the tree. I waited until they had returned to their hive, determined to capture them, and their honey with them. I blew smoke at them until they were stunned. All became calm. Then we cut a hole out of the tree.

We were filled with joy and astonishment to see the immense and wonderful colony of insects. There was a huge stock of honey, which the boys and I collected.

donkey was reassured by this and it drew near Fritz.

Fritz seized the opportunity to throw the rope around its neck. It ran off, frightened, but was soon checked by the cord. We provided both donkeys with plenty of good food to calm them. The flight of Grizzle had resulted in some good fortune! We called our new donkey Lightfoot, and Fritz quickly trained it and adopted it as his own.

One day, when Fritz was out with Lightfoot gathering acorns, he discovered some long leaves shaped like swords. He brought them home as playthings for his youngest brother Francis.

For a short time, Francis was highly amused with the sword-leaves and then, like all children, he grew tired of his new toys and threw them aside.

I examined the leaves more closely and found them to be made of long fibers. This was flax, and good for making clothes. We could make stockings, shirts, thread, and rope. Fritz and Jack immediately went off to gather more. Elizabeth would oversee the production of the cloth, and we would all help.

The next day, we began our work. We hurried to a marshy area and soaked the flax leaves in the water. This would make the stems soft and easy to peel. While it was soaking, we gathered wood, which we used to carve wheels and reels, and began to build a spinning wheel and loom. On this, Elizabeth could make thread and weave cloth during the next few months.

The rainy season was coming and the spinning would fill those many cold months to come.

The weather, which had been warm and calm, became gloomy. The sky was often darkened with clouds. We spent our time in finding food to store for the coming months, and in building shelter for our animals to weather the storms. We dug up a full supply of yams and roots to make bread, with plenty of coconuts and sweet acorns. As long as we had dug up the earth, we planted the last of our European corn and some palm trees. These would be watered by the rains and would sprout for us in the spring.

We also moved from our home in the branches to the spaces between the roots at the bottom of the tree. I built a shed with a tarred roof to save us from the rains. We stored our goods in the staircase inside the tree to keep them dry.

Yet the little shed could scarcely hold

us all. It was uncomfortable and, what's more, it smelled bad from the closeness of our animals. We were half choked with smoke every time we built a fire and drenched with rain when we opened the door. The shed had no window, and we wished for sunlight. For the first time since our disaster, we missed the comfortable houses of our dear country—but what could we do?

Though we were cold and cramped, we put our time to good use. Elizabeth spun. I was writing a journal recording the story of our shipwreck—which the reader is enjoying right now. Ernest copied the pages of the story in his fine, clear handwriting. Fritz and Jack spent their time drawing from memory the various plants and animals of the area. And one and all helped teach little Francis to read. We were content if a little uncomfortable.

However, we all agreed that we should never pass another rainy season in such a situation. But where could we go? Fritz now remembered his favorite book, *Robinson Crusoe*. "He is our best guide and model," Fritz said. "He cut himself a home out of solid rock. And he was alone. We are six. We can succeed!" We all thought it was a wonderful idea. We would pass this rainy season where we were, but never again. Next year, we would be prepared.

I can hardly describe our joy when, after many boring and gloomy weeks, the sky began to brighten, the sun to dry the wet earth, and the winds to calm. We left our dreary shed with joyful shouts. We quickly led the cattle to pasture and immediately began cleaning Falcon's Nest, which was covered with dead leaves but otherwise unharmed.

We were not so lucky with Tent House, however. The storms had beaten down the tent and carried away part of the sailcloth. The rest was covered with mildew. Our tub boat was smashed to pieces, but our handsome pinnace had been spared. Much of the gunpowder was wet and could no longer be used. That was indeed a great loss. It was of the utmost importance that we find winter quarters where our stores—our only wealth—would be safe.

But I suspected we would never be able to imitate *Robinson Crusoe*. He found a cave, but there was none like it here. We would have to spend years chipping at the rock to make ourselves even a small home. However, we could at least save the rest of the gunpowder by making a very small opening in the rocks. Fritz, Jack and I went off to try, taking with us pick-axes, chisels, hammers and iron levers.

We made so little progress the first day that, in spite of our courage, we were tempted to give up. We kept going, however. As we penetrated deeper, I was relieved to find that the stone was softer. It was more like dried mud, and we could dig it out with a spade.

After a few days of very hard work, we measured the opening and found we had already dug seven feet into the rock. Fritz removed the rocks and mud with a wheelbarrow and slowly built a terrace with them in front of the opening. I worked to enlarge the opening in the hard rock, and Jack, the smallest of the three of us, was able to get inside and cut away below. Suddenly, he bawled out, "Father, Fritz, I have pierced through!"

"Hah, hah, Jack is at his jokes again," I cried.

"No, no," Jack responded. "I've hit a hollow!"

I hurried to look and took hold of the iron bar Jack had been using as a tool. I enlarged the opening he had made. Beneath it was a huge cave, though it was too dark to see inside it. I quickly sent Jack to his mother to get some candles and report on what we had found. He returned with his mother

and two younger brothers. Then, we entered the cave, each carrying a candle.

The most beautiful and magnificent sight welcomed us. The sides of the cavern sparkled like diamonds, reflecting the light from our candles. Crystals of every length and shape hung from the top of our vault and decorated its walls. The floor was covered with a fine white sand, and the entire cave was thoroughly dry. We might have imagined ourselves in the palace of a fairy.

The children wanted to make this wonderful cave our new home immediately, but their mother and I disagreed. We would stay at Falcon's Nest for the good weather. We would use our time to cut windows in the cave and to build rooms using large planks of wood. We would also build a fireplace for a kitchen and indoor stables for the animals. This grotto would be our winter home.

Chapter 8

The Anniversary

One morning, having risen early, I occupied myself in counting up the time that had passed since our shipwreck. I found that the following day would be its anniversary. I decided that the event should be celebrated with all the pomp our situation would allow.

The next day, we dressed as well as we could in our scanty clothing. We would spend the time in song and play, with the boys competing in all kinds of games. The first contest would be shooting.

I set up a wooden marker, which we called a kangaroo. Jack did wonders, shooting away one of the ears of our pretend kangaroo! Then I threw a piece of cork in the air and the boys shot at it. Ernest did best, shooting the ball to pieces, but Jack could not hit it this time. I complimented all the boys on the progress they had made since last year.

Next came a running race, for which I gave them a course over Family Bridge and to Falcon's Nest. "The one that arrives first," I said, "will bring me, as

proof, my knife which I left on the table under the tree." I then gave the signal by clapping my hands. My three older sons set out, Jack and Fritz with all the speed they could. Ernest, who never did any-thing without thinking, ran slowly at first. He was being careful, and it might win him the race.

The runners were gone about three quarters of an hour. Jack returned first, but he was mounted on

the buffalo. The donkeys Grizzle and Lightfoot followed behind.

"What's this?" I said. "It was your legs and not those of the buffalo that I wished to exercise."

"Bah!" cried Jack. "I knew I would never get there first, so I left the course.

I guessed the riding race would be next, so I thought I would bring our mounts back with me."

Fritz came second, all out of breath and covered with sweat, but he didn't have the knife. It was Ernest who brought it to me.

"Fritz left first and arrived back before you—so how do you come to have the knife, Ernest?" I asked.

"It's simple," answered Ernest. "On the way there, Fritz couldn't keep up his fast pace and soon stopped for breath, while I ran on and got the knife. But in coming back, Fritz had learned a lesson. He paced himself as I had before. Since he's 16 and I'm only 13, he got here first." I praised both boys for their skill and declared Ernest the winner.

But now Jack, mounted on the buffalo, demanded that the riding exercises begin so he could make up for his loss. "To the saddle, to the saddle," he bellowed with all his force.

Fritz mounted Lightfoot, and Ernest took Grizzle. But although they tried, Jack beat them both. He was bold. To stop, charge, and turn was but a trifle to him. Just as I had declared the contest over and was about to proclaim Jack victor, little Francis rode into the arena, mounted on a young bull who was not more than three or four months old. My wife had made him a saddle.

"Gentlemen," said the little rider, saluting us with a pretend bow. "I haven't competed yet. Let me show you what I can do."

We all loudly applauded him as Francis began his show. The boy was more cool and calm than most his age. He had also managed to tame the bull quite completely, with help from Elizabeth, who looked on proudly. We all proclaimed Francis an excellent rider.

After the riding came swimming, climbing trees, and gymnastics. Then I announced that the rewards would be

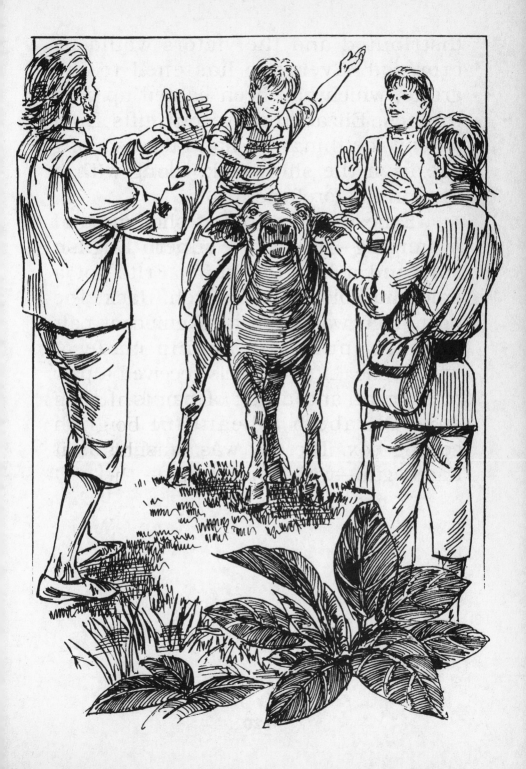

distributed and the victors would be crowned. Everyone hastened to the grotto, which had been lighted up with torches. Elizabeth gave out gifts from among the things we had taken so long ago from the shipwreck, along with a kiss on the forehead.

Ernest—conqueror at shooting and swimming—received a superb English rifle and a hunting knife. Fritz got a splendid gold pocket watch. Jack, the best rider, was given a magnificent pair of steel spurs and a whip made of whalebone. Little Francis received a pair of stirrups and a box of paints. I then gave Elizabeth a beautiful English sewing box. The day was finished as it had begun—with joyful songs.

Chapter 9

Our Second Winter

When a full season had again run its course, we found ourselves once more faced with the rainy season. But this year, we were far better prepared. We had spent the year cultivating crops of all sorts—potatoes, corn, wheat, rice, guavas, sweet acorns, pineapples, anise, and manioc plants. We had set up stores of meats. Our livestock would be well provided for in our warm, dry grotto.

The rains had already started by the time we finished all our work. The horizon became covered with thick clouds. The wind swept fearfully along the coast. The trees bent to the terrible blasts of wind. It seemed to us that the storms of last year had been nothing compared to this.

After two weeks, the winds began to calm. The rain fell more gently. But we knew it would keep up for twelve long weeks. At the beginning, we were sad at being stuck inside all day, but we soon began to arrange our new home cheerfully.

We made tables and chairs and lit our home with lanterns. We used mirrors everywhere to reflect the light, and soon the grotto was as bright as sunlight. Fritz and I worked together in the work-room. Jack helped his mother in the kitchen. Ernest and Francis arranged the books we had saved from the wreck into a library.

Among these books were works on history, botany, philosophy, voyages and travels, and grammars and dictionaries of different nations. There were also maps and a portable globe. We all knew German and a little French, from our native land of Switzerland. But we began to study English, the language of the sea, for I knew that most ships had at least a few sailors who spoke it. Jack also started learning Spanish and Italian. As for myself, I tried to master the Malay tongue, for the charts and maps convinced me we were in the neighborhood of these people.

Our grotto became so comfortable that the children couldn't think of any name they liked better than The Fairy Palace. But after a long discussion, we decided to call it "Felsenheim," which means "dwelling in the rock" in German, our native tongue.

Soon, the bad weather renewed itself. The rain, the winds, the thunder redoubled with fury. How happy we were in our home. What would have become of us in our high palace at Falcon's Nest?

But at last, the weather became calm. The clouds disappeared. The rain stopped. We were able to leave our grotto. We walked up the stretch of rocks along the coast and took pleasure in climbing the highest peaks. Then we emptied out the rain from the canoe I had made before winter and explored some more. On an island in the middle of the bay, we found an enormous whale lying on the beach.

Our whale looked like those of

Greenland. The back was greenish black, the stomach yellowish, and the fins and tail black. It was about sixty or seventy feet long. Its eyes were not much larger than those of an ox.

Fritz and Jack entered the head of the whale and cut out the whalebone from the mouth. Meanwhile, Ernest and I collected the whale's blubber. We could use the fat for oil to make light and heat.

But we were soon joined by birds, which were also attracted to the whale. They flew round and round our heads. Soon, they were boldly snatching pieces of blubber from our hands. When we had taken all we wanted, we abandoned the rest of the whale to them. Everything was placed in our canoe and we set sail for Felsenheim with our precious new cargo.

The next day, we strained the whale blubber for oil, then cooked the rest of it to get out as much oil as possible. We worked far from Felsenheim because of the terrible odor.

Later, Elizabeth suggested making a new colony on Whale Island, as we had begun to call it. "We'll put some fowls there," she said. "They'll be safe from the monkeys and the jackals. We can also plant some sugarcane and some roots on the island." I liked the idea very much, and so did the children.

But rather than working when we arrived on the island, the children ran off to the beach to gather shells. Elizabeth and I were left to put her plan into action.

Meanwhile, Fritz and Ernest had discovered a monstrous turtle. It was too big for them to turn over, and Ernest was struggling with it, holding onto one of its legs. It was about to escape when I arrived. Using spikes as levers, Fritz and I were able to turn the turtle on its back.

It was about eight and a half feet long and couldn't weigh less than five hundred pounds. I didn't know how we'd be able to carry it home. Then it came to me. "Zounds!" I said, striking my forehead. "We won't carry the turtle home, we'll let *it* carry *us*."

We tied reins to the the turtle's shell and attached barrels to its back so it couldn't dive underwater and draw us down with it. Then we tied the canoe to the turtle and it led us home. Ernest compared us to Neptune, the sea god, gliding over the waves drawn by dolphins. We arrived safely at Felsenheim.

Chapter 10

A Dangerous Visitor

One day, from outside our grotto we saw a cloud of dust arise from the direction of Falcon's Nest. Fritz, whose eagle eye was always making discoveries, said, "There is some large animal there. I can see it plainly. It has a greenish-colored body. What do you think it is, Papa?"

I ran for the spyglass and looked toward the dust. "A serpent—a huge serpent coming directly for us!"

"Shall I run for the guns?"

"No. We must get to safety. The serpent is too powerful for us to attack it from here."

We hurried to the entry of the grotto and prepared to meet our enemy. It was a boa constrictor. We watched it stretch its enormous length along the bank of the river. From time to time, it would raise up the front part of its body off the ground, and turn its head as if seeking prey. It darted its triple-barbed tongue from its half-open jaws.

The serpent crossed Family Bridge, and headed straight for the grotto. We barricaded the door and the windows. We passed our muskets through the door, and waited silently for the enemy. It was a silence of terror.

The boa stopped about thirty paces from our home. Ernest, more out of fear than anger, fired his gun. Elizabeth, Jack, and Francis followed his example.

The serpent raised its head, but either none of the shots had touched it or the scales of its skin were too tough. It glided away with unbelievable speed, toward the marsh where our ducks and geese lived, and soon it disappeared in the rushes.

Fear of the serpent kept us shut up for three days—three long days of fear and alarm. We knew it hadn't left yet because each evening the whole colony of ducks and geese would sail away for Whale Island, where it was safe. We were in a terrible state, until Grizzle, our poor old donkey, came to our aid.

Grizzle got loose and pushed open the door. He shot off like an arrow, and was away in the open plain before we could stop him. It was a comical sight to see him kicking his heels in the air. Fritz would have mounted Lightfoot and ridden out after Grizzle, but I wouldn't let him. I tried to coax Grizzle back by calling his

name and blowing our cow-horn, but it was useless. He ran directly towards the swampy marsh.

Horror froze our veins when we saw the awful serpent emerging from the rushes! It raised its head, darted out its forked tongue, and crawled quickly toward the donkey. Poor Grizzle soon saw the danger and began to run, braying with all his might. But neither his cries nor his legs could save him.

We uttered cries of terror. Our donkey was dead. We had heard its last bray. Afterwards, the serpent lay perfectly still and asleep.

I saw that the time had come, and finally I exclaimed, "Now, my children, now the serpent is in our power!"

Fritz, Jack, Ernest, and I set out from the grotto carrying our guns. The serpent raised its head and, throwing me a look of powerless anger, let it fall again. We advanced nearer and fired our pistols. The serpent lay dead upon the sand before us, stretched out like the mast of a ship.

Chapter 11

A New Land

We had nothing more to fear from the boa, but I was afraid it might have left behind a mate or a nest of little ones. These could spread terror through our lands. I decided to take a trip through the passage in the rock, where I supposed the boa had gotten through. We set out loaded with our hunting gear.

We passed through the gap in the rocky cliff that marked the edge of the land we had explored so well. We had been that way only once before—when we had almost been trampled by a herd of buffaloes. We could easily trace the spiral track of the boa in the sand. Later, I intended to build a solid wall here so that no other serpents or dangerous animals could get through.

As we traveled, we recognized the place where we had taken the buffalo. As we advanced farther, the plants became fewer and fewer until we found ourselves in the middle of an immense desert. The sun beat down on our heads and the sand burned our feet.

After two hours of painful walking, we arrived at the foot of a hill. Because it was so high, it offered a little shade. There, we rested from the overpowering rays of the sun and ate a small meal to keep up our strength.

But we didn't rest for long. Soon Fritz spied something moving. Great, graceful birds—ostriches! We agreed to capture one and bring it home. It would look beautiful among our domestic animals. We hid behind some large tufts of a plant and waited for the ostriches to come our way.

But our dogs sprang forward and attacked them. Away flew the birds, as fast as a bundle of feathers being blown by the wind. Their feet seemed not to touch the ground and their wings looked like sails. But the dogs kept after them and attacked the largest bird, a male. We ran to save him but when we arrived, he was already dying from the wounds the dogs had given him.

We were sorry for what had happened, but could do nothing about it. We pulled the white tail feathers from the dead ostrich and placed them proudly in our hats. The rich feathers contrasted with our old, worn-out beaver hats, but they were excellent protection against the rays of the sun.

Jack and Ernest went on ahead of Fritz and me. Soon they seemed to make some great discovery, for we saw them waving their plumed hats and heard them shouting to us to hurry.

"A nest!" they cried. "An ostrich nest! Quick! Quick!"

We ran to them and found the two boys standing over a large hole in the ground. In it were some twenty-five to thirty eggs, each as large as a child's head. My sons wanted to hatch them by exposing them to the rays of the sun, and then wrapping them up as warmly as possible at night.

I replied that each of the eggs weighed about three pounds and that we were already so loaded down we could hardly drag our knapsacks across the desert. Besides, the sun's warmth would never replace the care of the adult ostriches. But the children insisted. Each took one egg.

We walked until we passed from the desert into a great swamp. We could see in the distance troops of buffaloes, monkeys, and antelopes. There were no signs of any boas. We stopped at this marsh and refreshed ourselves with some food. We also filled our empty gourds with water.

We left the borders of the swamp to return home, following a little stream of water. It led us through an oasis in the desert, filled with trees and grass. How delicious this route was compared with our painful journey of the morning.

But scarcely had we gotten comfortable when Ernest, who had walked on ahead, let out a terrible cry. I heard two howls. The dogs barked. A moment later, Ernest appeared running, his face pale. He cried out in a voice stifled with fear, "Bears! Bears! They're following me." And the poor boy fell into my arms. I myself was seized with a sudden shiver as an enormous bear appeared, immediately followed by a second.

"Courage, children," was all I could say. I seized my gun and prepared to fight.

We fired, wounding the bears but not killing them. The dogs fought

bravely, too, rolling in the dust with the bears. We would have fired again, but we were afraid we would hit the dogs. We crept closer. About four paces from the bears we fired. The huge animals fell back motionless on the sand.

We drew the bears into a nearby cave and covered them with thorn bushes to keep off the beasts and birds of prey. We also buried our ostrich eggs in the sand. They were too heavy to carry, and this would keep them safe until we could pick them up the next day. Then, we continued on our way home.

The sun had set when we rejoined my dear Elizabeth and little Francis. A very good fire and a well-cooked supper refreshed our weary bodies. My little heroes told the long story of our day's adventures. Jack made up for the small share he'd had in our story by boasting and swaggering enough for all.

We returned to the cave the next day to skin the bears for the fur. I divided the meat into long strips, which we smoked. We left the remains for the birds of prey, who soon picked the bones so clean that there remained nothing but two perfectly white skeletons. These we carried home with us for our museum. As for the ostrich eggs, Ernest made cups out of them.

In the cave, I also found several minerals, including a superb block of talc, as transparent as glass. I decided to turn it into window panes for our home. Ernest helped me and we soon cut off a splendid piece big enough for our job. We would divide it into leaves no thicker than paper. Elizabeth was overjoyed. Anything that reminded her of Switzerland made her happy.

It had taken us most of the day to do all this. As night approached, we gathered around our fire, where Elizabeth was cooking stew. The smell that escaped from the pot promised us a delicious supper.

All that was left to complete this adventure was the building of a solid wall across the gap in the rocks where the snake had come through. It was hard work, and it occupied us for more than a month. When we relaxed from our work, the boys would wander off and always bring us home something useful.

It was not too many days later

when Fritz suggested a new project. We should build a fort on Shark Island in case of danger. His head was so full of plans that it was impossible to say no, and we soon began the work.

Our goal was to bring the two cannons we had saved from the ship to the island, build a platform more than fifty feet high, and mount them there.

But how would we raise up the cannons? We built a tall tower on top of the platform and attached a long rope, tied the cannons on and hauled them up.

This work cost us a whole day of hard labor. At last, the cannons were mounted, their mouths pointing toward the sea. We placed a long pole in the rock, with a string and pulley, so we could sail a flag.

How proud we felt! We uttered a cry of joy. Even though we had to save our gunpowder, we made a special celebration and fired our cannons six times. The rocks and the ocean echoed with the sound.

Chapter 12

A Great Treasure!

It is with amazement that I look at the number of pages I have written. Every day I write even more. Ten years have passed away since we were thrown on this coast. Each year was much like the last. We had our fields to sow, our harvests to gather, and our home life to attend to. It was our good luck to land in one of the most lush and beautiful lands on the planet. We were always able to provide for all our needs. But we still missed our homeland, our own dear Switzerland.

Over the years, we made many improvements. In front of our grotto, we built a gallery with a roof that rested on columns made of light bamboo. Vines of vanilla and pepper grew up the columns, making them as picturesque as a Chinese pavilion.

Shark Island was no longer a dry bank of sand. We had planted palm and pineapple trees everywhere and the earth was a carpet of green. Our Swiss flag floated gaily in the breeze atop the flagpole of our fort.

Our gardens and plantations had grown tremendously. Between the grotto and the bay was a grove of trees and shrubs as beautiful as an English garden. Our European trees had grown with incredible speed, but their fruits had lost their flavor. Perhaps it was not the right kind of soil or perhaps it was the salt air, but the apples and pears became black and withered. On the other hand, the native plants thrived—bananas, figs, guavas, oranges, and lemons made our island a complete paradise. We lacked for nothing—if only we could have found other people!

My sons were no longer children. Fritz was twenty-five years of age—not tall, yet very strong from all the exercise.

Ernest was twenty-two, healthy but not as broad as his older brother. He had always loved to study and was now a well-informed young man, smart and bright. Jack was as headstrong at the age of twenty as he had been at ten. He was the strongest and the quickest. Francis was sixteen. He was solid and tall, agile, and skillful. They were all honest, good-hearted men. My dear Elizabeth did not seem to have grown old. As for me, my hair had become whitened by age—what little was left. But I still *felt* young.

One day, Fritz gave us a great scare. He went off in his canoe and traveled far out to sea. As night approached, nothing could be seen of him. Elizabeth was in a state of great terror.

I set out after him in the pinnace, heading for Shark Island. From there, we fired an alarm-cannon. A few moments later, we saw a black spot in the far distance. We looked through the spyglass and saw Fritz's craft. He moved slowly, beating the sea with his oars, as if his canoe were very heavy.

Soon, he had returned to us, safe and sound. He announced, "I have made a discovery worth more to us than all the treasures of the earth!"

Fritz brought on shore his sack and recounted his adventures. "The weather was beautiful and the waves peaceful," he began. "Seabirds flew around me uttering piercing cries. Sea lions, sea elephants, and walruses played on the rocks, bellowing frightfully. I passed into a magnificent bay with clear waters. At the bottom were beds of large oysters, much bigger and better than the ones we have gathered here at home. But when I opened some to try them, I didn't find a nice, fat oyster but only some little round, hard stones, like peas. They were pearls! I filled a little box with them."

I examined the stones. "You have discovered a treasure, my son," I agreed.

Fritz continued, "As I started to leave the bay, marine animals about the size of calves began to plunge and frisk around my boat. I was afraid they would upset it, so I attacked the first one that came near me. The others fled. The animal's skin was thick and I thought it would be useful. I jumped onto a nearby rock and began to skin it. But while I was doing this, seabirds clustered around me. They came so close that I whirled my staff around to keep them away. In doing so, I knocked down a large bird—an albatross. I loaded the skin into my boat and returned home."

All rejoiced at his safe return. But when my wife and younger boys went off to unload the animal skin from the boat, Fritz drew me aside and confided a secret in my ear.

"Something very important happened on my voyage," he said. "The albatross I knocked down had a piece of linen tied around one of its feet. On it were written the English words, 'Save the poor ship-wrecked sailor on the rock.' I can't express to you, father, what I felt. I read and re-read the words to make sure I wasn't dreaming. From that moment, my only thought has been to save the sailor!

"I wrote another note and attached

the linen back on the albatross. The note said, 'Help is near!' If the bird returns to the place it came from, the sailor can read my answer.

"If we should find the unfortunate one, what joy, what happiness! And yet, what despair if we don't succeed! That's why I didn't tell my brothers and my mother, to spare them the agony if we should fail."

"You have acted wisely," I said. "And I'm glad you didn't go immediately to look for the sailor—you'll need help and provisions. As for our chances of success, the albatross is quite a traveler. The linen might have been put on its foot thousands of miles from here, or years ago. But we will certainly try."

Chapter 13

A Rescue

My three older boys and I prepared for a voyage—Jack and Ernest suspecting only that we were going to harvest more of the pearls.

We loaded the canoe and pinnace with hams, cassava cakes, barley-bread, rice, nuts, almonds, dried fruits and barrels of water, plus many tools. Our dogs—the children of our original companions Turk and Flora—came with us. There was a fresh and favorable breeze. We embarked immediately.

We steered our way through the rocks with great difficulty. The rocks were covered with the whitened bones of walruses. Ernest made us stop several times so he could collect some of the remains for our museum of natural history. At last, we arrived at the bay of pearls. We used rakes, hooks, nets and poles to gather a large quantity of the precious oysters. We made ready to go back to Felsenheim.

But as we were turning toward home, Fritz paddled up to me in his canoe, handed me a paper, and shot off like an arrow. I opened the paper. It said that he was going in search of the shipwrecked sailor. It was unsafe to go alone, but Fritz rowed so fast that he was soon out of sight.

Five days passed and still Fritz had not returned. His mother was so worried that we all went in search of him. We had not gone far when Ernest uttered a loud scream. "Fritz!" he cried, and pointed to a vessel in the distance dancing over the waves. Nearer and nearer he came. At last, we were together.

When we had freed Fritz from our many embraces, we asked him all sorts of questions, speaking all together. I drew him aside and demanded to know if he had been successful concerning the sailor. He said eagerly and joyously, "I was, papa. I found the poor shipwrecked girl—for it was a woman who had written those lines. For three years she lived on a little island all alone, without anything. Oh, but don't say anything to the others. I want to enjoy their surprise."

I told my family to hoist the sails, weight anchor, and make ready to leave. It took us an hour to sail to the island. The young woman was waiting for us there. She was dressed as a handsome young sailor and she had timid eyes.

It had been such a long time since we had seen another human being—ten years!—that we were speechless.

The silence was broken by Fritz who, taking the young sailor by the hand, said, "May I introduce you to Emily Montrose. She, like ourselves, has been shipwrecked on this coast." His voice broke with emotion.

"She is welcome among us," said Elizabeth joyfully. I assured Emily she would always find food and warmth with us. My wife and I would be her parents, and my sons her brothers. Elizabeth

opened her arms and Emily rushed into them, bursting into a flood of tears and thanking us for our kindness.

Joy now reigned among us. Supper was served—it was a great treat to Emily. My sons asked the shy newcomer so many questions she didn't know who to answer first. But they were also embarrassed and awkward. My poor boys didn't know how to act with a young lady—they had never met one before.

We loaded up the things Emily had saved from her shipwreck and those she had made herself—clothes, ornaments, utensils, and tools. Emily now said goodbye to the island that had been her home for three years. We turned toward Felsenheim.

We were curious about Emily's story. She was English, but raised in India. Her mother had died when she was young. Her father had taught her how to shoot and ride as well as how to sew. He was a colonel in the navy and, when they wanted to return home to England, she was not allowed to sail on his navy ship—for such were the rules. She did, however, sail on the same day as he did, but in another ship.

A terrible storm arose. The ship was thrown off course and a rough wave drove it onto our rocky coast. The poor girl alone escaped the waves, which carried her to land. The first few days, she felt nothing but despair. She had no food except some birds' eggs, which she found in the rocks. But over time, she built a hut, fished, hunted, and tamed birds—but she was alone for three long, dreary years.

As we neared home, the boys took one boat and sailed on ahead so they could have everything prepared for Emily

when we returned. They greeted us with a ten-gun salute. The moment Emily's foot touched the sand, a hurrah echoed through the air. In the grotto, a table was spread with bananas, figs, guavas, oranges, fried fish, and a huge turkey. A wreath of flowers spelled out, "Welcome, fair Emily!" Emily, for her part, was astonished that a single family could have accomplished so much. Then, she sat down happily at the table.

In the days and weeks that followed, Emily proved her worth. She worked as hard as any of us, and always with zeal and industry. She inspired everybody. Emily became to Elizabeth and myself a fifth child, and a beloved sister for my sons.

Chapter 14

Conclusion

I have a thousand different feelings as I write the word *Conclusion*. It was toward the end of the rainy season and a patch of blue sky could now and then be seen. We opened the door of our home and breathed fresh air.

Our first care was for our gardens, which had been damaged during the winter. Then Jack and Fritz set out for Shark Island to check on our fort. Nothing important had been destroyed there. To make sure the cannons were in good order, they began firing.

They were astonished when, a moment later, they heard three shots of a cannon in the distance! But they didn't know who had fired so they hurried home to tell the rest of us.

"If there is really a ship on our coasts," I said, "who knows whether it's manned by honest sailors or pirates? Should we rejoice or be sorry? Should we prepare to be saved or attacked?"

To be safe, I quickly created a defense. Fritz and Jack were impatient and decided to return to Shark Island to try a new signal. I went with them. On arriving at the fort, we hoisted our flag and Jack loaded a cannon and fired it. Then, we heard a louder answering shot in the direction of Cape Disappointment.

Jack couldn't contain his joy. "People! It's people!" he cried, dancing about us.

Overpowered with emotion, we hurried to our boat to explore the mysterious shot. We coasted along without

seeing anything, and almost began to think we'd imagined it all. Then we rounded a spit of land and, suddenly, we beheld a fine ship majestically resting at anchor. An English flag floated at the masthead.

I cannot find the words to express the feelings which filled us. Fritz wanted to throw himself into the sea and swim to the ship. I was afraid that, even with the English flag, the ship might be full of pirates who flew the flag in order to deceive others. I cried out through my speaking-trumpet these three words: "Englishmen, good men!"

But there was no answer. Perhaps *they* were afraid of *us*. Our clothes marked us as natives, possibly unfriendly ones. We wished to present ourselves in a better light, so we darted off as fast as our boat could carry us.

We spent a whole day preparing for our meeting and loading our craft with gifts. We set off at sunrise. When we could

see the ship again, I cried, "Hoist the English flag!" We approached the ship to welcome it to our shores.

The captain received us with openness and friendship. I recounted the history of our shipwreck and our stay on the coast. I told him of Emily and asked if he had ever heard of her father. He not only knew him but assured me that he was alive and well.

He told me that his ship, on its way to Sydney, had been blown off course. "When we heard your cannon, we wondered who was unfortunate enough to be stuck on this coast. Instead, we find an organized colony, filled with everything anyone could need." This made us laugh and we took the captain's hand in friendship.

When we prepared to return to shore, the captain asked us to take with us an English family—Mr. Wolston and his wife and two daughters—who were not well.

My readers can imagine how astonished the Wolston family was upon seeing everything we'd accomplished. The two families united over a dinner meal under the gallery of the grotto, and my wife prepared beds for the newcomers inside Felsenheim's rocky vaults.

The next morning, Mr. Wolston came to me with tenderly outstretched hands and spoke as follows: "Sir," said he, "we have been admiring the wonders here. You live happily, far from the difficulties of the world. I came from England seeking rest. Where can I find it better than here? I would be the happiest of men if you would allow us to stay."

This idea of Mr. Wolston's filled me with joy and I immediately assured him that we would share half of everything we had with his family.

The morning was devoted to the joy and pleasure that this news caused. But sadness also occupied my mind. The ship was the only one we'd seen in ten years and probably as long a time would go by before another appeared. Should we let the captain and his ship leave without us?

Elizabeth didn't wish to return to Europe. I was myself too attached to my new life to leave it. But our children were young. I didn't want to deprive them of civilization. And Emily, since she had heard her father was in England, wanted badly to return.

At last, I called my children together and asked them if they would leave with the captain's ship or be happy to remain the rest of their lives on this coast. Jack and Ernest said they would stay. Ernest needed nothing more than his books and a quiet place to study, which he had here. Jack enjoyed hunting too much to go. Fritz and Francis, however, had a great desire to return to Europe.

The Wolston family, too, was split up. One daughter remained with her parents. These arrangements were very painful.

The ship remained eight days at anchor. We prepared rich cargo for our children to take with them—pearls, ivory, spices, and furs. We also furnished the ship with meat and fruits.

On the eve of their departure, I had one last conversation with my children. I gave Fritz the diary I had written of our shipwreck and life on the coast, which you read now. None of us slept much during the last night. At dawn, the cannon of the ship announced that all who were leaving must board. We brought our children to the shore. There, we embraced them one last time.

e anchor had been weighed, the
unfurled, the flag run up the
thead, and a rapid wind promised
separate us from our loved ones
quickly. I will not try to describe the
grief of my dear Elizabeth. Jack and
Ernest are weeping bitterly and I, too,
can but badly conceal my sorrow.

I finish these lines while the ship's
boat is waiting. My sons receive my last
blessing. Good-bye, dear children!
Good-bye, Europe. Good-bye, Switzerland.
Never shall I see you again. May you
always be happy, good-hearted and free!

THE END

ABOUT THE AUTHOR

Johann David Wyss was born in Switzerland in 1743. Brought up in a religious family, Wyss eventually became a pastor in the city of Bern.

Wyss made up the story of *Swiss Family Robinson* to tell his four sons. As the story grew day by day, Wyss began to write it down. He and his son, Johann Emmanuel, illustrated it together.

Another son, Johann Rudolf, grew up to be a professor and scholar of Swiss folklore. Years later, he completed his father's unfinished manuscript.

Swiss Family Robinson was finally published in two parts, in 1812 and 1813. It was translated into English in 1814 and is one of the most popular novels ever written. Wyss died in 1818 at the age of 75.

Treasury of Illustrated Classics™

Adventures of Huckleberry Finn
The Adventures of Robin Hood
The Adventures of Sherlock Holmes
The Adventures of Tom Sawyer
Alice in Wonderland
Anne of Green Gables
Black Beauty
The Call of the Wild
Gulliver's Travels
Heidi
Jane Eyre
The Legend of Sleepy Hollow
& Rip Van Winkle
A Little Princess
Little Women
Moby Dick
Oliver Twist
Peter Pan
Rebecca of Sunnybrook Farm
Robinson Crusoe
The Secret Garden
Swiss Family Robinson
Treasure Island
20,000 Leagues Under the Sea
The Wizard of Oz